THE CYCLE OF THOUGHT

NAPOLEON HILL'S
THE CYCLE OF THOUGHT

A Book to Inspire Your Positive Self

Napoleon Hill and Judith Williamson

An Approved Publication of The Napoleon Hill Foundation

Published 2019 by Gildan Media LLC
aka G&D Media
www.GandDmedia.com

NAPOLEON HILL'S THE CYCLE OF THOUGHT. Copyright 2012, 2019 The Napoleon Hill Foundation.

No part of this book may be used, reproduced or transmitted in any manner whatsoever, by any means (electronic, photocopying, recording, or otherwise), without the prior written permission of the author, except in the case of brief quotations embodied in critical articles and reviews. No liability is assumed with respect to the use of the information contained within. Although every precaution has been taken, the author and publisher assume no liability for errors or omissions. Neither is any liability assumed for damages resulting from the use of the information contained herein.

Front Cover design by David Rheinhardt of Pyrographx

Interior design by Meghan Day Healey of Story Horse, LLC

Library of Congress Cataloging-in-Publication Data is available upon request

ISBN: 978-1-7225-0113-6

10 9 8 7 6 5 4 3 2 1

Introduction

Napoleon Hill's *The Cycle of Thought*—a book to inspire your positive self.

This upside down book replicates the cycle of thought. Positive thinking does not just "happen," but often occurs in tandem with the outgrowth of negative thought. If not for loss, a person might not be able to appreciate a gain in finances, relationships, and employment among many other circumstances in life. In order to focus on the good the bad needs to be acknowledged. This cyclic balance demonstrates the ebb and flow of the Universe constantly in motion both for and against itself.

Replication exists throughout nature and so too in individual lives. It has been stated that "What we think about we bring about." This upside down book will aid you in seeing the opposite side of many situations and serve as a counter balance to the negative thinking that may confront you each and every day.

As you work through this book, remind yourself that it is ultimately you who creates your end result. Whether it is a blessing or a curse depends upon the system of unconscious habits that you create. These habit programs run your life whether you admit it or not. Being entirely positive or entirely negative is not a realistic approach to life. A person must see the "bad" in order to see the "good." One cannot exist without the other. Dr. J. B. Hill, grandson of Dr. Napoleon Hill, states:

Of course, we have to do more than think positively.

To do otherwise is to proceed blindly along some chosen pathway. For example, negative thinking allows us to provide a framework of problems that need to be solved and anticipate new problems. Imagine some General that pushes his attack forward without worrying about danger to his flanks or logistical tail. How successful will HE be? Understanding ourselves must also include understanding our weaknesses. Our thinking must be multivariate.

When a person begins to understand how the thought process works, he or she can then begin to work on the habits that produce the desired outcomes in life. If you want the desired picture perfect end result you need to install the software program—or habits—that take you to a life well lived.

Be Your Very Best Always, Judith Williamson, Director: Napoleon Hill World Learning Center, Purdue University Calumet

Directions

This book can be read two ways: right side up or upside down. Imagine as you read that you have a "bad angel" and a "good angel" sitting respectively on your left and right shoulders.

The bad angel may advise you to behave one way and the good angel another. Let's let one represent a negative thought and the other a positive thought. In keeping with Dr. Hill's philosophy and acknowledging that change does not take place overnight but is a steady progression of small, consistent, daily actions, you can begin to chart a course of improvement for yourself when you identify the two endpoints. First you must know where you are before you can create a roadmap to a new destination. In a similar manner, to move from a negative thought to a positive one requires that a person knows which is which. This book will help you identify non-constructive or even damaging thoughts and then help you move toward more positive ones.

Daily, read the thoughts and let them seep into your mind. Perhaps you might decide to read them at morning, noon, and night. As you discern the negative approach to the topic, the opposing positive thought will give you an alternative route.

Perhaps you would like to journal briefly about the topic as well. This will give you insight into both the negative and positive approaches. Sometimes, a person only recognizes that they are stuck when they begin to notice the landscape is not changing around them. To become unstuck one must first admit that no movement has occurred.

Use this book as a prompt for change. One or two simple revelations can change your entire life. By reading and considering the negative and positive thoughts, you can locate a place within yourself that allows you to move toward an improved version of the life you live.

Be Your Very Best Always,
Judith Williamson

Day 1

You should know I control 98 percent
of the people of your world.

Ninety-eight percent of the people in the world are drifting though life with no plan or purpose. This is the major cause of failure.

Day 1

Day 2

I consist of negative energy, and I live in the minds of people who fear me.

Keep your mind on the things you want and off the things you don't want.

Day 2

Day 3

I also occupy one-half of every atom of physical matter and every unit of mental and physical energy.

Day 3

Success attracts success and failure attracts failure because of the law of harmonious attraction.

Day 4

Perhaps you will better understand my nature if I tell you I am the negative portion of the atom.

Don't overlook small details. Remember that the universe and everything in it is made of atoms, the smallest known particles of matter.

Day 4

Day 5

The other half is occupied by my opposition. The opposition is what you earthbound call God.

The orderliness of the world of natural laws gives evidence that they are under the control of a universal plan.

Day 6

It is my business to represent the negative side of everything, including the thoughts of you earthbound people.

Day 6

The subconscious has one very peculiar trait. It believes everything everyone tells it, and acts accordingly. It believes and acts on your spoken words, and it believes in and acts on your thoughts. Use your subconscious to serve you in everything you do.

Day 7

My opposition controls positive thought.
I control negative thought.

Man is the only living creature equipped with the power of choice through which he may establish his own thought and behavior patterns. You have the power to break bad habits and to create good ones in their place—at will.

Day 8

I sow the seeds of negative thought in the minds of people so I can occupy and control the space!

Day 8

Taking possession of your positive self will put you on the success beam that you may ride triumphantly to whatever heights of achievement you desire.

Day 9

I plant the seed of fear in the minds of people, and as these seeds germinate and grow, through use, I control the space they occupy.

Day 9

You are the master of your destiny. You can influence, direct and control your own environment. You can make your life what you want it to be.

Day 10

The six most effective fears are:
the fear of poverty, criticism, ill health,
loss of love, old age, and death.

Some people are never free from troubles, mainly because they keep their minds attuned to worry. The mind attracts that which it dwells upon.

Day 10

Day 11

The first and the last of the six fears—
poverty and death—serve me most often.

Close the door of fear behind you, and see how quickly the door to success opens in front of you.

Day 12

I plant these fears in the minds of people so deftly that they believe them to be their own creation.

Worry is a state of mind based upon fear. It works slowly but persistently. It's insidious and subtle. Step by step it "digs itself in," until it paralyzes one's reasoning faculty and destroys self-confidence and initiative. Worry is a form of sustained fear caused by indecision—therefore it is a state of mind that can be controlled.

Day 13

I accomplish this end by making people believe I am standing just beyond the entrance gate of the next life, waiting to claim them after death for eternal punishment.

Kill the habit of worry in all its forms by reaching a firm decision that nothing life has to offer is worth the price of worry. With this decision will come poise, peace of mind, and calmness of thought—which will bring happiness.

Day 14

Of course I cannot punish anyone, except in that person's own mind, through some form of fear—but fear of the thing that does not exist is just as useful to me as fear of that which does exist.

Faith is a state of mind that you can attain only by clearing your mind of negative thoughts and conditioning it to receive positive thoughts.

Day 15

All forms of fear extend the space
I occupy in the human mind.

Only you can keep you down!
You and only you have complete control
of your mind. This is a basic truth of life.
It follows, therefore, that you are the only
one who can set limitations for yourself.

Day 16

I gained control over a million years ago
when the first man began to think.

There are no such realities as good or bad luck.
Everything has a cause that produces
appropriate effects.

Day 16

Day 17

Up to that time I had control over all mankind,
but enemies of mine discovered the power
of positive thought, placed it in the minds of men,
and then began a battle on my part to
remain in control.

Take possession of your own mind, and you may
soon make life pay off on your own terms.

Day 18

So far, I have done quite well by myself, having lost only two percent of the people to the opposition.

Whatever you possess, material, mental or spiritual, you must use it or lose it.

Day 19

My favorite physical dwelling place, as I have told you, is the minds of the earthbound.

If you are unhappy with your world and want to change it, the place to start is with yourself. If you are right, your world will be right. This is what PMA is all about. When you have a Positive Mental Attitude, the problems of your world tend to bow before you.

Day 20

I control a part of the brain space
of every human being.

Whine about your misfortunes and thereby
multiply them, or keep still and starve them out.

Day 21

The amount of space I occupy in each individual's mind depends upon how little, and what sort of thinking that person does.

Instead of worrying about the bad things that might happen to you, spend a few minutes every day enumerating the pleasant events that are going to happen.

Day 22

My opponent controls all the positive forces of the world, such as love, faith, hope and optimism.

Your mental attitude gives your entire personality a drawing power that attracts the circumstances, things and people you think about most.

Day 23

My opponent also controls the positive factors of all natural law throughout the universe, the forces which keep the earth and the planets and all the stars balanced in their courses, but these forces are meek in comparison with those which operate in the human mind under my control.

All physical and mental power is achieved through concentration of energy, which in turn is achieved only through self-discipline. If you can learn to control your thoughts, you will be able to control your deeds. This is self-discipline.

Day 24

You see, I do not seek to control stars and planets.
I prefer the control of human minds.

Day 24

Only if you have an open mind can you grasp the full impact of the first rule of the Science of Success: Whatever the mind can conceive and believe, the mind can achieve.

Day 25

I add to my power by appropriating the mind-power of the earthbound, as they come through the gate at the time of death.

Day 25

Success is the knowledge with which one may get all that he needs without violating the rights of his fellowmen or compromising with his own conscience.

Day 26

Ninety-eight out of every 100 who come back to my plane from the earth plane are taken over by me and their mind-power is added to my being.

Day 26

If you hesitate or turn backward while under fire you're not a fighter—you're a quitter. And, the devil himself hates the person with a rubber backbone because he smells bad burning.

Day 27

I get all who come over with any form of fear.

Keep your thoughts focused and positive! Your mind acts like an electromagnet to attract the things upon which you keep it focused. You have the power (and the right) to control your thought habits, thereby using this power in your behalf.

Day 28

You see I am constantly at work, preparing the minds of people before death, so I can appropriate them when they come back to my place.

Day 28

Take possession of your own mind and worry will have to find another boarding house.

Day 29

I have countless ways of gaining control of human minds while they are still on the earth plane.

It's impossible to erase the mistakes of the past, but you can recognize them and learn from them. You can decide to change the effect they have on the way you think and act. "Life either rides you, or you ride it." Decide today to learn from your past, and not to let your past ride you.

Day 30

My greatest weapon is poverty.

Day 31

I deliberately discourage people from accumulating material wealth because poverty discourages men from thinking and makes them easy prey for me.

People who are determined to attain success start where they stand, make the best of whatever tools they have and acquire whatever else they need along the way. Start from wherever you stand—today!

Day 32

My next best friend is ill health.
An unhealthy body discourages thinking.

Day 33

All who inspire people to think and act on their own initiative are my enemies.

Day 33

If I had one wish that would be granted for the asking, I would ask for more wisdom.

Day 34

Poverty is always my friend because it discourages independence of thought and encourages fear in the minds of men.

Day 34

The only limitations you have are the ones you set in your own mind.

Day 35

Some wealthy men serve my cause while others do me great damage, depending upon how the wealth is used.

If you have something you don't need, give it to someone who needs it. It will come back one way or another.

Day 36

Any habit which weakens one's willpower invites a flock of its relatives to move in and take possession of the mind.

Day 37

I ask no person to believe in me.
I prefer that people fear me. I am no beggar!
I take what I want by cleverness and force.
Begging people to believe is the business
of my opposition; not mine.

You can't become the master of anything until you become the master of your own ego.

Day 38

I get what I want by exercising self-control. It is not so good for my own business, but I suggest you emulate me instead of criticizing me.

You have to be bold and wise enough to ask of life more than you may think you are worth. It is an observable fact that people tend to rise to meet demands that are put on them.

Day 39

I have so many devices for entering
human minds and controlling them that
it is difficult to say which are the most powerful.
Right at the moment I am trying to bring
about another world war.

Men take on the nature and the
power of thought of those with whom they
associate in a spirit of sympathy and harmony.

Day 39

Day 40

If I can start the world to killing on a wholesale basis I shall be able to put into operation my favorite device for mind control. It is what you call mass fear.

Day 40

Hope is the raw material with which you build success. It crystallizes into faith, faith into determination, and determination into action.

Day 41

I could not control 98 percent of the people
of the world if all people were skilled
in thinking for themselves.

Power is organized knowledge
expressed through intelligent efforts.

Day 42

For millions of years I have dominated earthbound creatures through fear and ignorance.

Trouble is only opportunity in work clothes.

Day 43

I will speak first of the principle of habit, through which I silently enter the minds of people.

Nothing ever just happens. You have to make things happen, including individual success. Success is the direct result of definite action, carefully planned and persistently carried out by the person who has conditioned his mind for success and believes he will attain it.

Day 44

By operating through this principle I establish the habit of (I wish I could avoid using this word) drifting.

You can never stand still. You must move upward toward success—or downward toward failure. The choice is yours alone.

Day 45

When a person begins to drift on any subject he is headed straight toward the gates of what you earthbound call hell.

Personal initiative is the inner power that starts all action. It is the dynamo that spurs the faculty of your imagination into action and inspires you to finish what you start. Personal initiative is self-motivation.

Day 46

I can best define the word "drift" by saying
that people who think for themselves never drift,
while those who do little or no thinking
for themselves are drifters.

Day 47

A drifter is one who permits himself to be influenced and controlled by circumstances outside of his own mind.

That which you think today becomes that which you are tomorrow.

Day 48

A drifter is one who accepts whatever Life throws in his way without making a protest by putting up a fight. He doesn't know what he wants from life, and spends all of his time getting just that.

Knowledge is not power. It is potential power that becomes real through use.

Day 49

A drifter has lots of opinions, but they are not his own. Most of them are supplied by me.

You will never be free until you learn to do your own thinking and gain the courage to act on your own personal initiative.

Day 49

Day 50

A drifter is one who is too lazy mentally to use his own brain. That is the reason I can take control of people's thinking and plant my own ideas in their minds.

Your success or failure is in your own mind!

Day 51

Sometimes I lay the foundation for my control of a mind before the owner of it is born, by manipulating the minds of that person's parents.

Many parents make life hard for their children by trying too zealously to make it easy for them.

Day 52

Sometimes I go further back than this and prepare people for my control through what you earthbound call "physical heredity."

Thinking good thoughts, positive and cheerful thoughts, will improve the way you feel. What affects your mind also affects your body.

Day 53

I help to bring people into your world with weak brains by giving to them, before birth, as many as possible of the weaknesses of their ancestors. You call this principle "physical heredity."

Be thankful for the adversities that have crossed your pathway, for they have taught you tolerance, sympathy, self-control, perseverance and some other virtues you might never have known.

Day 54

After people are born I make use of what you earthbound call "environment" as a means of controlling them. This is where the principle of habit enters.

You are where you are because of your habits of thought!

Day 55

The mind is nothing more than the sum total of one's habits.

Day 56

I enter the minds of people through thoughts which they believe to be their own. Those most useful to me are fear, superstition, avarice, greed, lust, revenge, anger, vanity and plain laziness.

The conscience speaks, not in audible words, but through that small voice that comes from within.

Day 56

Day 57

I induce them to drift through school without knowing what occupation they wish to follow in life.

All your successes and failures are the result of habits you have formed.

Day 58

Habits are related. Drift in one direction and soon you will be drifting in all directions.

Some people have learned to use the winds of adversity to sail their ship of life.

Day 59

I take possession of people during their youth, before they come into possession of their own minds, by using those who are in charge of them.

Thought, whether accurate or inaccurate, is the most highly organized functioning power of your mind. You are but the sum total of your dominating or most prominent thoughts.

Day 60

Once I capture the mind of a child through fear,
I weaken that child's ability to reason and
to think for himself, and that weakness goes
with the child all through life.

Day 60

Misfortune has a habit of showing up
where it's expected.

Day 61

Might is right with me. I use every known human weakness to gain and keep control of the human mind.

Remember your mental limitations are of your own making.

Day 61

Day 62

I cause children to become drifters by following the example of their parents, most of whom I have already taken over and bound eternally to my cause.

Before anything can come out of a mind, something must be put in. Successful people never stop acquiring specialized knowledge related to their major purpose.

Day 63

In some parts of the world I gain mastery over children's minds and subdue their will power in exactly the same way that men break and subdue animals of lower intelligence.

Your progress in life begins in your own mind and ends in the same place.

Day 64

It makes no difference to me how a child's will is subdued, as long as it fears something.

Never underestimate the repellent power of a Negative Mental Attitude. It can prevent life's lucky breaks from benefiting you. A Positive Mental attitude attracts good luck.

Day 65

I will enter its mind through that fear and limit the child's power to think independently.

Day 65

Give your children your praise rather than your condemnation, because it is human nature for people to live up to the reputation that others give them.

Day 66

Accurate thought is death to me.

Accurate thought involves two fundamentals. First, you must separate facts from mere information. Second, you must separate facts into two classes—the important and the unimportant. Only by so doing can you think clearly and accurately.

Day 67

I cannot exist in the minds of those who think accurately. I do not mind people thinking as long as they think in terms of fear, discouragement, hopelessness and destructiveness.

Accurate thinking depends on two fundamentals: Inductive Reasoning, based on assumption of unknown facts or hypotheses when the facts are not available; and Deductive Reasoning, based on known facts or what are believed to be facts.

Day 68

When they begin to think in constructive terms of faith, courage, hope and definiteness of purpose, they immediately become allies of my opposition, and are therefore lost to me.

Your subconscious mind often works out your greatest problems when your conscious mind is asleep. Be sure to always "feed" your subconscious positive thoughts!

Day 69

I live in fear that someday some courageous person will reverse the present system of school teaching and deal my cause a death blow by allowing the students to become the instructors, using those who now serve as teachers only as guides to help the children establish ways and means of developing their own minds from within.

Day 70

School children are taught, not to develop and use their own minds, but to adopt and use the thoughts of others.

When the six departments of the mind (Ego, Emotions, Reason, Imagination, Conscience, and Memory) are guided and coordinated by self-discipline, you will be able to negotiate your way through life with a minimum of opposition from others.

Day 71

I cause people to drift on every subject through which I can control independent thought and action.

The greatest of all riches is just plain common sense.

Day 71

Day 72

Take the subject of health, for example.
I cause most people to eat too much food
and the wrong sort of food.

You are a mind with a body!
Since your brain controls your body,
know that sound physical health is dependent
upon a Positive Mental Attitude.

Day 73

I cause men and women to drift into marriage without plan or purpose designed to convert the relationship into harmony.

Dreams are not born of indifference, laziness or lack of ambition. The dreamer must take off with a burning desire to be and to do before his dreams will ever be a reality.

Day 74

I teach people to become drifters by causing them to drift out of school into the first job they can find, with no definite aim or purpose except to make a living.

Day 74

Decide what kind of person you want to be, and develop positive traits by emulating others you admire. Replace bad habits with good ones and focus your mind on positive thoughts.

Day 75

I cause people to spend freely and to save sparingly or not at all, until I take complete control of them through their fear of poverty.

To master yourself, you must first master your habits; otherwise they will quickly master you.

Day 76

I cause people to drift into inharmonious and unpleasant environments in the home, in their places of occupation, in their relationship with relatives and acquaintances, and to remain there until I claim them through the habit of drifting.

A rudderless ship and a purposeless person are eventually stranded on desert sand.

Day 77

I cause people to drift into the habit
of thinking negative thoughts.

I feel healthy! I feel happy! I feel terrific!
Commit to start each day with a positive
affirmation of yourself, your life, and your job.

Day 78

I plant the seeds of negative thought in the minds of people through the pulpit, the newspapers, the moving pictures, the radio and all other popular methods of appeal to the mind.

Your brain is both a broadcasting station and a receiving station for vibrations of thought, both positive and negative.

Day 79

I cause people to allow me to do their thinking for them because they are too lazy and too indifferent to think for themselves.

Don't allow a Negative Mental Attitude to make you a loser.

Day 80

Any habit which causes one to procrastinate—
to put off reaching a definite decision—
leads to the habit of drifting.

Deeds, not mere words. If you are really smarter than others you will let others find this out from your deeds.

Day 81

Man alone defies nature's laws
and drifts when he wills.

Make yourself indispensable in your job and see
how quickly you're pushed into a better job.

Day 82

I control the minds of men solely because of their habit of drifting, which is only another way of saying that I control the minds of men only because they neglect or refuse to control and use their own minds.

Your world will change whether or not you choose to change, but you have the power to choose its direction.

Day 83

There are no self-appointed dictators. I appoint them all. Moreover, I manipulate them and direct them in their work.

Like attracts like. Every thought, feeling and emotion held in your conscious mind has the tendency to draw to it thoughts, feelings and emotions of a similar nature. So be careful what you send out!

Day 84

My dictators do no drifting. That is why they rule for me the millions of people under their control.

Your reputation is that which people think you are; your character is that which you are.

Day 84

Day 85

I am paying each of them with the sop of his own vanity, by making him believe he is acting on his own account.

In every soul there has been deposited the seed of a great future, but that seed will never germinate—much less grow to maturity—except through the rendering of useful service.

Day 86

Right now I am paving the way for a dictatorship by sowing the seeds of fear and uncertainty in the minds of the people.

Day 86

Fear is the most costly of all the human emotions, even though most fears have no foundation in fact.

Day 87

Drifting is the most common cause of failure in every walk of life.

No one who is unwilling to make personal sacrifices achieves success.

Day 88

I can control anyone who I can induce
to form the habit of drifting on any subject.

Sow an action and you reap a habit;
sow a habit and you reap a character;
show a character and you reap a destiny.

Day 89

First, the drifter is just so much putty in my hands, to be molded into whatever pattern I choose, because drifting destroys the power of individual initiative.

Two kinds of people never get ahead: those who do only what they are told to do and those who will not do what they are told. Your employer does not control the quality of service you render. You control that, and it's the thing that makes or breaks you.

Day 90

Second, the drifter cannot get help from my opposition, because the opposition is not attracted to anything so soft and useless.

Day 90

Education means development of the mind so that it will work for you and not against you. All education is self-acquired because no one can educate another.

Day 91

Poverty, like physical illness,
is a contagious disease.

Man is master of his fate because he is master of his attitude. No more effort is required to aim high in life, to demand abundance and prosperity, than is required to accept misery and poverty.

Day 92

It may mean something to you when I call your attention to the fact that the non-drifters which I do not control, and those who possess most of the wealth of the world, happen to be the same people.

We are all born equal in the sense that we all have equal access to the Great Principle: the right to control our thoughts and mental attitude.

Day 92

Day 93

Men who know how to get the material things of life generally know how to keep out of the hands of the Devil as well.

Think about the fact that you have complete control over but one thing—the power of your own thoughts. You can clear the mental cobwebs of negative passions, emotions, feelings, tendencies, prejudices, beliefs and habits by consciously developing their positive opposites.

Day 94

The ability to acquire things is contagious.
Drifters acquire nothing except
that which no one else wants.

Direct your thoughts with PMA to control
your emotions and to ordain your destiny.

Day 94

Day 95

If more people had definite aims and stronger desires for material and spiritual riches I would have fewer victims.

Day 95

A Positive Mental Attitude . . . PMA . . . is a can-do and will-try attitude. It is the right, honest, constructive thought, action or reaction to any person, situation or set of circumstances.

Day 96

I have control over no non-drifter,
present or past. I control the weak,
not those who think for themselves.

Day 97

The first thing you will notice about a drifter is his total lack of a major purpose in life.

If you study the lives of those who have done anything constructive, you will find an uncompromising belief in oneself and a refusal to accept defeat.

Day 98

A drifter will be conspicuous by his lack of self-confidence.

Believe in yourself—first and foremost! What you believe yourself to be, you are. The attitudes you transmit to others will tell more about yourself than the words you say or how you look.

Day 99

A drifter will never accomplish anything requiring thought and effort.

To become an expert achiever in any activity, it takes: practice, practice, practice!

Day 100

A drifter spends all he earns and more too, if he can get credit.

One bad habit often spoils a dozen good ones.

Day 100

Day 101

A drifter will be sick or ailing from some real or imaginary cause, and calling to high heaven if he suffers the least physical pain.

Day 101

If your mind can make you sick—and it can—remember, it can make you well, too!

Day 102

A drifter will have little or no imagination.

You have the power to create anything you can imagine! Act on the ideas produced by your imagination . . . you will achieve success!

Day 103

A drifter will lack enthusiasm and initiative to begin anything he is not forced to undertake, and he will plainly express his weakness by taking the line of least resistance whenever he can do so.

Be dependable, be willing to assume responsibilities, be on hand always, be loyal, be courteous, be willing to help others get ahead, and you will be practically sure to become financially independent.

Day 104

A drifter will be ill-tempered and lacking in control over his emotions.

Change your mental attitude and the world around you will change accordingly.

Day 104

Day 105

A drifter's personality will be without magnetism and it will not attract other people.

Your personality can be your greatest liability or asset. It embraces everything you control: mind, body, and soul.

Day 106

A drifter will have opinions on everything but accurate knowledge of nothing.

Day 107

A drifter may be jack of all trades
but good at none.

You can always tell a man who thinks he is smarter than others, but you can't tell him much.

Day 108

A drifter will neglect to cooperate with those around him, even those on whom he must depend for food and shelter.

Cooperation is the beginning of all organized effort.

Day 109

A drifter will make the same mistake over and over again, never profiting by failure.

You cannot achieve enduring success in any worthy undertaking until you become big enough to blame yourself for your own mistakes and reverses.

Day 110

A drifter will be narrow-minded and intolerant on all subjects, ready to crucify those who may disagree with him.

Day 111

A drifter will expect everything of others but be willing to give little or nothing in return.

It is more profitable to be a go-giver rather than a go-getter.

Day 112

A drifter may begin many things
but he will complete nothing.

Day 113

A drifter will be loud in his condemnation of his government, but he will never tell you definitely how it can be improved.

An opinion is no sounder than the judgment of the person offering it.

Day 113

Day 114

A drifter will never reach decisions on anything if he can avoid it, and if he is forced to decide he will reverse himself at the first opportunity.

Day 114

I refuse to believe what you say unless it harmonizes with what you do.

Day 115

A drifter will eat too much and exercise too little.

Follow work with play, mental effort with physical, eating with fasting, seriousness with humor, and you will be on the road to sound health and happiness. Don't try to cure a headache. It's better to cure the thing that caused it.

Day 116

A drifter will take a drink of liquor
if someone else will pay for it.

Always follow the Golden Rule:
Do unto others as you would
have others do unto you.

Day 117

A drifter will gamble if he can do it "on the cuff."

You will never get to where you want to be on dead hopes or hopeful wishing.

Day 117

Day 118

A drifter will criticize others who are succeeding in their chosen calling.

One way to avoid criticism is to do nothing.

Day 119

In brief, a drifter will work harder to get out of thinking than most others work in earning a good living.

Do it now . . . and before anyone tells you to do it!

Day 120

A drifter will tell a lie rather than
admit his ignorance on any subject.

All rivers and some people are crooked because
they follow the path of least resistance.

Day 121

If he works for others, a drifter will criticize them to their backs and flatter them to their faces.

Day 121

Only two people in every hundred know precisely what they desire from life and have a workable plan for attaining their goals. These are the leaders, the success stories we hear of every day. Isn't it odd that these people have no more opportunities than the other 98?

Day 122

The first sign of a non-drifter is this: He is always engaged in doing something definite, through some well-organized plan which is definite.

Failure comes from drifting, success from persistent climbing. With persistence you will win.

Day 123

The non-drifter has a major goal in life toward which he is always working, and many, minor goals all of which lead toward his central scheme.

Day 123

Initiative, built on a definite understanding of what must be achieved, puts one in harmony with everyone around him, and with the universe as a whole.

Day 124

The tone of his voice, the quickness of his step, the sparkle in his eyes, the quickness of his decisions clearly mark the non-drifter as a person who knows exactly what he wants and is determined to get it, no matter how long it may take, or what price he must pay.

How can you maintain a Positive Mental Attitude? By thinking and acting on the can do part of every plan and refusing to accept as insurmountable the no can do part that can be found in almost every undertaking.

Day 125

If you ask the non-drifter questions he gives you direct answers, and never falls back on evasions or resorts to subterfuge.

A genius is someone who has taken full possession of his own mind and directed it toward objectives of his own choosing, without permitting outside influences to discourage or mislead him.

Day 126

The non-drifter extends many favors to others,
but accepts favors sparingly or not at all.

A man's best recommendation is that which he gives himself by rendering superior service, in the right mental attitude.

Day 127

The non-drifter will be found up front whether he is playing a game or fighting a war.

Day 127

Personal initiative is the quality that impels a person to do that which ought to be done without his being told to do so.

Day 128

If the non-drifter does not know
the answers he will say so frankly.

An educated person is not necessarily
the one who has the knowledge, but the one
who knows where to get it when needed.

Day 128

Day 129

The non-drifter has a good memory;
he never offers an alibi for his shortcomings.

It is not necessary for others to fail
that you may succeed.

Day 129

Day 130

The non-drifter never blames others for his mistakes no matter if they deserve the blame.

Day 130

When everyone else fails you in times of adversity, try depending on yourself and you may discover hidden riches of fabulous value in your own mind power.

Day 131

The non-drifter used to be known as a go-getter, but in modern times he is called go-giver.

The more you share, the more you will have.

Day 131

Day 132

You will find the non-drifter running the biggest business in town, living on the best street, driving the best automobile, and making his presence felt wherever he happens to be.

Day 133

The non-drifter is an inspiration to all who come into contact with his mind.

The world pins no medals on you because of what you know, but it may crown you with glory and riches for what you do.

Day 134

The major distinguishing feature of the non-drifter is this: He has a mind of his own and uses it for all purposes.

Mental "dynamite" is anything that causes the mind to start the wheels of the imagination turning.

Day 135

The major difference between the drifter
and the non-drifter is something equally available
to both. It is simply the prerogative right of each
to use his own mind and think for himself.

The successful person budgets time,
income and expenditures, living within his
means. The failure squanders time and income
with a contemptuous disregard for their value.

Day 136

I would admonish the non-drifter
to wake up and give!

Day 137

The drifter should be admonished
to give some form of service useful
to as many people as possible.

Day 138

The non-drifter is supposed to give.
He must give before he gets!

If it isn't your job to do it,
perhaps it's your opportunity.

Day 139

I am powerless to influence or control
you because you have found the secret approach
to my kingdom. You know that I exist only
in the minds of people who have fears.

People refuse to take chances in business
because they fear the criticism that may follow
if they fail. The fear of criticism in such cases
is stronger than the desire for success.

Day 140

You know that I control only the drifters who neglect to use their own minds.

One of the major causes of personal failure is the lack of persistence in carrying through that which one begins.

Day 140

Day 141

You know that my hell is there on earth and not in the world that comes after death.

Infinite Intelligence recognizes no limitations except those we impose on ourselves.

Day 142

You know that I am a principle or form of energy which expresses the negative side of matter and energy, and that I am not a person with a forked tongue and a spiked tail.

Day 143

You know that you can release all of my earthbound victims whom you contact, and this definite knowledge is the blow with which you will deal me the greatest damage.

Keep your conscious mind focused on what you want, and your subconscious mind will unerringly guide you to it.

Day 144

I cannot control you because you have discovered your own mind and you have taken charge of it.

Don't look to the stars for the cause of your misfortunes. Look to yourself and get better results.

Day 145

Flattery is one of my most useful weapons. With this deadly instrument I slay the big ones and the little ones.

The more you discipline yourself, the less you will be disciplined by others. Sound character provides the power with which a person may ride the emergencies of life instead of being overwhelmed by them.

Day 146

Flattery is a bait of incomparable value
to all who wish to gain control over others.

Day 147

Flattery has powerful pulling qualities because it operates through two of the most common human weaknesses: vanity and egotism.

Actions, not words, are the greatest means of self-praise.

Day 148

There is a certain amount of vanity and egotism in everyone. In some people these qualities are so pronounced they literally serve as a rope by which one may be bound. The best of all ropes is flattery.

Day 148

All you can take with you at the end of your life is whatever you have added to your character—good and bad.

Day 149

Flattery is the chief bait through which men seduce women. Sometimes; in fact, frequently women use the same bait to gain control of men especially men who cannot be mastered through sex appeal.

You have two types of energy. One is physical; the other is mental and spiritual. The latter is by far the more important, for from your mind you can draw vast power and strength in time of need.

Day 150

Flattery is the chief bait with which my agents weave their way into the confidence of people from whom they procure information needed to carry on warfare.

Don't cry about loss—God never takes anything away without replacing it. Think positive, especially in times of difficulty!

Day 151

Wherever anyone stops to feed his vanity on flattery I move in and begin to build another drifter. Non-drifters are not easily flattered.

Education comes from within; you get it by struggle and effort and thought.

Day 152

I inspire people to use flattery in every human relationship where its use is possible because those who are influenced by it become easy victims of the drifting habit.

Learn to motivate others by example.

Day 153

Age has nothing to do with one's susceptibility to flattery. People respond to it, in one way or another, from the time they become conscious of their own existence until they die.

Emotions are not always reliable. You can protect yourself against emotions by carefully examining and weighing them through the power of reason and the rules of logic.

Day 154

A woman can be most easily flattered by telling her that she is pretty, or that she wears clothes well.

It is always safe to talk about others as long as you speak of their good qualities.

Day 155

The most effective motive in harpooning men is egotism, with a capital E!

Congratulate yourself when you reach that degree of wisdom which prompts you to see less of the weaknesses of others and more of your own, for you will then be walking in the company of the really great.

Day 156

Tell a man he has a strong Herculean body, or that he is a great business tycoon, and he will purr like a cat and smile like an opossum!

Your personality reveals a great deal about who and what you are. It reveals how you think, your ethical standards, the kind of life you lead. You can develop a pleasing personality by developing a sincere and honest love for other people.

Day 156

Day 157

All men are not equally susceptible to flattery. Two out of every 100 men have their egotism so thoroughly under control that even an expert flatterer couldn't get under their skins with a double edged butcher knife.

Every word you speak advertises your wisdom or ignorance. Remember this before speaking. Communication is the basis for getting along with others.

Day 158

Women influence men through a technique consisting, first, of the ability to inject soft, cooing baby tones into their voices, and, second, by closing their eyes into a half-closed position which registers hypnotism in connection, with the flattery of men.

One little word—"please"—carries the power of great charm.

Day 159

The type of woman who uses flattery never sells a man herself or anything she can give him. Instead she sells him his own egotism.

Your mental attitude is the most dependable key to your personality.

Day 160

The majority of people begin to drift as soon as they meet with opposition, and no one out of ten thousand will keep on trying after failing two or three times.

The only way you will achieve success is to organize your thought power and direct it to the end you desire.

Day 161

Failure breaks down one's morale, destroys self-confidence, subdues enthusiasm, dulls imagination and drives away definiteness of purpose.

Every great achievement is born out of struggle.

Day 162

Search accurately into the lives of men and women who achieve enduring success and you will find, without exception, that their success has been in exact proportion to the extent that they surmounted failure.

Day 163

The life of every successful person loudly acclaims that which every true philosopher knows: "Every failure brings with it the seed of an equivalent success."

Struggles are necessary. They are nature's way of allowing you to expand, develop, progress, and become stronger. The one thing nature will not tolerate is idleness! If you don't like the circumstances of your life—change them!

Day 164

This seed springs to life only when it is in the hands of one who recognizes that most failures are only temporary defeat, and never, under any circumstances, accepts defeat as an excuse for drifting.

Day 164

The person who is tempered by hardship becomes a stronger person who can do more for himself and more for others.

Day 165

Failure is a virtue only when it does not lead one to quit trying and begin drifting.

Day 166

I induce as many people as I can to fail
as often as possible for the reason that no one
out of ten thousand will keep on trying
after failing two or three times.

If you can look at problems as temporary
setbacks and stepping-stones to success, you
will come to believe that the only limitations
you have are the ones in your own mind.

Day 167

I am not concerned about the few who convert failures into stepping stones because they belong to my opposition anyway. They are non-drifters and therefore they are beyond my reach.

Failure is a blessing or a curse, depending on whether you react to it as a stumbling block or a stepping-stone. The nature of your reaction is under your exclusive control.

Day 168

One of my most effective tricks
is known to you as propaganda.

Your mind has been endowed with
the power to think, to aspire, to hope,
to direct your life toward any goal.

Day 169

My propagandists cover the world
so thoroughly that I can start epidemics
of disease, turn loose the dogs of war or
throw business into a panic at will.

Day 170

Propaganda is any device, plan, or method by which people can be influenced without knowing that they are being influenced, or the source of the influence.

People seldom begin to succeed until they are past 40, mainly because most of their early years are spent in un-learning things that aren't true.

Day 171

What is fear of the devil except propaganda? I never attain an end by direct, open means, which I can achieve through subterfuge and subtlety.

Your mind is the one and only thing over which you have the complete, unchallenged privilege of control.

Day 171

Day 172

I make my first entry into an individual's mind by bribing him.

Both poverty and riches are the offspring of thought.

Day 173

I use many things as bribes, all of them pleasant things the individual covets.

Happiness is an elusive, transitory thing. And if you set out in search of it, you will find it evasive. But if you try to bring happiness to someone else, then it comes to you.

Day 174

My best bribes are: love, the thirst for sex expression, covetousness for money, the obsessive desire for something for nothing-gambling, vanity in women, egotism in men, desire to be the master of others, desire for intoxicants and narcotics, desire for self-expression through words and deeds, desire to imitate others, desire for perpetuation of life after death, desire to be a hero or a heroine, and desire for physical good.

Every man takes care that his neighbor does not cheat him. But a day comes when he begins to care that he does not cheat his neighbor. Then all goes well, for he has changed his market cart into a chariot of the sun.

Day 175

I go to work immediately to occupy as much of a person's mind as I can master.

Attend well to your character, and your reputation will look out for itself.

Day 176

If an individual's greatest weakness is the desire for money I begin to dangle coins before him, figuratively speaking.

Review your own life. Are you balancing work with play, mental effort with physical effort, seriousness with humor?

Day 177

I intensify a person's desire for money,
and induce him to go after money. Then when
he gets near it I snatch it away from him.

If you don't save anything, you are absolutely sure never to be financially independent no matter how great your income.

Day 178

After the trick has been repeated a few times the poor fellow gives in and quits. Then I take over a little more space in his mind and fill it with the fear of poverty.

If you're not learning while earning, you're cheating yourself of the better portion of your just compensation.

Day 179

If my victim converts his desire for money into large sums I start overfeeding im with the things he can buy with it.

Day 179

If you make your prayers an expression of gratitude for the blessings you have received instead of requests for what you don't have, you will see results much faster.

Day 180

For example, I cause him to stuff himself with rich foods. This slows down his thinking capacity, endangers his heart and starts him on the road to drifting.

Day 180

You can enjoy good health! A Positive Mental Attitude will attract good health; a Negative Mental Attitude will attract ill health.

Day 181

If the victim is male I can usually snare him through his sex appetite. Over-indulgence in sex starts more men to drifting toward failure than all other causes combined.

You can't separate your body from your mind. Whatever affects the body will affect the mind; whatever affects the mind will affect the body.

Day 182

Why, do you suppose, rich men's sons seldom equal the achievements of their fathers? I'll tell you why. It is because they have been deprived of the self-discipline which comes from being forced to work.

The greatest cure for loneliness, discouragement and discontentment is work that produces a healthy sweat.

Day 183

I use for the purpose of bribery the things all people naturally desire, but the non-drifter resembles a fish that steals the bait from your hook but refuses to take the hook.

Do not settle for anything short of what you want.

Day 184

The non-drifter takes from life whatever he wants, but he takes it on his own terms.

As long as you are willing to let life push you around, it will.

Day 184

Day 185

The drifter takes whatever he can get,
but he takes what he gets on my terms.

Day 185

The law of compensation isn't always swift,
but it is as certain as the setting of the sun.

Day 186

The non-drifter borrows money
from a legitimate banker, if he wants it,
and pays a legitimate rate of interest.

The person who plans his day in advance
goes about his work logically and efficiently.
When there is no organization of schedule,
there is no place to begin.

Day 187

The drifter goes to the pawn shop, hocks his watch and pays a suicidal rate of interest for his loan.

Day 188

Protection against drifting lies within easy reach of every human being who has a normal body and a sound mind.

The successful person is open-minded and tolerant on all subjects.

Day 189

Do your own thinking on all occasions. The fact that human beings are given complete control over nothing save the power to think their own thoughts is laden with significance.

If you close your mind, you will be shut off from the recognition of favorable opportunities and the friendly cooperation of others.

Day 190

Decide definitely what you want from life, then create a plan for attaining it and be willing to sacrifice everything else, if necessary, rather than accept permanent defeat.

Opportunity generally takes up with those who recognize it. If you can see an opportunity as quickly as you can see the faults of others, you will soon be rich.

Day 191

Analyze temporary defeat, no matter of what nature or cause, and extract from it the seed of an equivalent advantage.

Put your mind to work.
Assess your ability and energy.

Day 192

Be willing to render useful service equivalent to the value of all material things you demand of life, and render the service first.

Day 192

Who could use your help? How can you help? It doesn't take money . . . all it takes is ingenuity and a strong desire to be of genuine service. Helping others to solve their problems will help you to solve your own.

Day 193

Recognize that your brain is a receiving set that can be attuned to receive communications from the universal store house of Infinite Intelligence, to help you transmute your desires into their physical equivalent.

When faith is blended with thought, the subconscious mind instantly picks up the vibration, translates it into its spiritual equivalent and transmits it to Infinite Intelligence.

Day 193

Day 194

Recognize that your greatest asset is time, the only thing except the power of thought which you own outright, and the one thing which can be shaped into whatever material things you want.

Time is endless. Your opportunity to use time is temporary. Make the best use of both to achieve success.

Day 195

Budget your time so none of it is wasted.

The most costly words in the English language are "I don't have time." You can budget your time correctly to have time for all your needs.

Day 196

Recognize the truth that fear generally is a filler with which the Devil occupies the unused portion of your mind.

The seven basic fears include the fear of poverty, criticism, ill health, loss of love, old age, loss of liberty, death.

Day 197

Fear is only a state of mind which you can control by filling the space it occupies with faith in your ability to make life provide you with whatever you demand of it.

Since fear is merely a state of mind, you can control it by taking action.

Day 198

When you pray, do not beg! Demand what you want and insist upon getting exactly that with no substitutes.

You must believe that what you want will happen, and you must take the necessary action to ensure it.

Day 199

Recognize that life is a cruel taskmaster. That you either master it or it masters you.

Day 200

Never accept from life, anything you do not want. If that which you do not want is temporarily forced upon you, you can refuse, in your own mind, to accept it and it will make way for the thing you do want.

Day 201

Remember that your dominating thoughts attract, through a definite law of nature, by the shortest and most convenient route, their physical counterpart. Be careful what your thoughts dwell on.

The Law of Harmonious Attraction: Like attracts like; success attracts more success; failure attracts more failure. Make use of this law by always keeping your attitude positive.

Day 202

Be definite in everything you do and never leave unfinished thoughts in the mind. Form the habit of reaching definite decisions on all subjects.

Day 203

The habit of drifting can be broken
if the victim has enough will-power,
providing it is done in time.

Day 203

Don't be like a ship at sea without a rudder, powerless and directionless. Decide what you want, find out how to get it, and then take daily action toward achieving your goal.

Day 204

There is a point beyond which the habit can never be broken. Beyond that point the victim is mine.

Day 205

The victim resembles a fly that has been caught in a spider's web. He may struggle, but he cannot get out.

It's more likely that you will rust out your brain from disuse than wear it out from overuse.

Day 205

Day 206

The web in which I entangle my victims permanently is a law of nature not yet isolated by, or understood by, men of science.

All things are possible to the person who believes they are possible.

Day 206

Day 207

Any impulse of thought the mind repeats over and over through habit, forms an organized rhythm.

If you direct your thoughts and control your emotions, you will ordain your destiny.

Day 208

Undesirable habits can be broken.
They must be broken before they assume
the proportions of rhythm.

Take charge of your life.
You are what you think!

Day 209

Rhythm is the last stage of habit!
Any thought or physical movement
which is repeated over and over through
the principle of habit finally reaches
the proportion of rhythm.

You must learn how to control your
thoughts before you can control your deeds.
Any power, mental or physical, is achieved
through concentration of energy, which, in
turn, is achieved only through self-discipline.

Day 210

When the habit reaches the proportion of rhythm it cannot be broken because nature takes it over and makes it permanent.

Day 211

It is something like a whirlpool in water. An object may keep floating indefinitely unless it is caught in a whirlpool. Then it is carried round and round but it cannot escape.

Opportunity, before crowning you with great success, usually tests you with adversity to see what sort of mettle you're made of.

Day 212

All I have to do to gain control over
any mind is to induce its owner to drift.

No one who is unwilling to make personal sacrifices achieves great success. All positive habits are the product of willpower directed toward the attainment of definite goals.

Day 213

Those who control and use
their own minds escape my web.

Day 214

The human fear that best serves
my purpose is the fear of death.

Day 215

No one can prove definitely what happens after death. This uncertainty frightens people out of their wits.

When enthusiasm comes in the front door, worry runs out the back door.

Day 216

Every attack made against me fixes the fear of me in the minds of all who are influenced by it.

Day 217

My only worry is that someday
a real thinker may appear on earth.

The creative force of the entire universe functions
through your mind when you establish a definite
purpose and apply your faith to its fulfillment.

Day 217

Day 218

If this happened, people would learn
the greatest of all truths—that the time they
spend in fearing something would, if reversed,
give them all they want in the material world
and save them from me after death.

Render more and better service than that
for which you are paid and sooner or later
you'll receive compound interest on
compound interest from your investment.

Day 219

It may interest you to know that the fear of criticism is the only effective weapon I have with which to whip you.

No one has yet discovered the limitations of the power of the mind, because there are none.

Day 220

If the world ever produces an accurate thinker with ability to fathom the deeply buried secret of life and death you can be sure that science will be responsible for the catastrophe.

The best job goes to the person who can get it done without passing the buck or coming back with excuses.

Day 220

Day 221

You of course know that no one can be hypnotized by another person without his willingness to be hypnotized.

The power of autosuggestion is so great that it can render the word "impossible" so impotent that eventually it will become obsolete in your vocabulary.

Day 222

Neither can nature place one
under the spell of hypnotic rhythm
without his willingness to be hypnotized.

Your position is nothing more than your opportunity to show what sort of ability you have. You will get out of it exactly what you put into it—no more and no less.

Day 223

The willingness may assume the form of indifference toward life generally, lack of ambition, fear, lack of definiteness of purpose, and many other forms.

Day 224

Nature does not need one's consent in order to place him under the spell of hypnotic rhythm. It needs only to find him off guard, through any form of neglect to use his own mind.

Meet the most important living person! That person is you. Your success, health, happiness, and wealth depend on how you use your Positive Mental Attitude.

Day 225

Remember this: whatever you have
you use it or you lose it!

Count the day lost if the setting sun
finds you with no good deeds done.

Day 225

Day 226

All successful attempts to break the habit of drifting must be done before nature makes the habit permanent, through hypnotic rhythm.

Most failures could have been converted into successes if someone had held on another minute or made one more effort.

Day 227

Nature uses hypnotic rhythm
to make one's dominating thoughts
and one's thought habits permanent.

Patience + Persistence + Perspiration = Success

Day 228

Poverty is a disease because nature makes it so by fixing permanently the thought-habits of all who accept poverty as an unavoidable circumstance.

Day 229

Through this same law of hypnotic rhythm nature will also fix permanently positive thoughts of opulence and prosperity.

All enduring success begins with a success consciousness backed by a definite plan.

Day 230

If your mind fears poverty
your mind will attract poverty.

The most important ingredient
of success is belief in yourself.

Day 231

If your mind demands opulence and expects it, your mind will attract the physical and financial equivalents of opulence. This is in accordance with an immutable law of nature.

Your capacity to believe is your greatest potential asset.

Day 232

Life pays the drifter its own price, on its own terms. The non-drifter makes Life pay on his own terms.

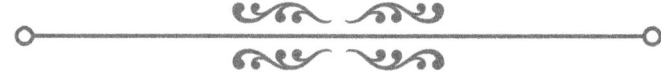

Day 233

You are where you are and what you are because of your own thoughts and your deeds.

Learn to fix your attention on a given subject, at will, for whatever length of time you choose. You will have learned the secret to power and plenty. This is concentration.

Day 234

Circumstances which people do not understand are classified under the heading of luck. Back of every reality is a cause.

Every man who holds a big job got there through luck. All he did was to cultivate a pleasing personality; made himself well liked by others; sowed seeds of kindness and good cheer wherever he went; rendered the most and best service of which he was capable. Luck did the rest.

Day 235

Often the cause is so far removed from the effect that the circumstance can be explained only by attributing it to the operation of luck. Nature knows no such law as luck.

Successful people have their time thoroughly organized, with every minute budgeted and directed to the ends of their own choosing.

Day 235

Day 236

The terms luck and miracle are twin-sisters.
Neither of them has any real existence except
in the imaginations of people.

Day 237

Everything having a real existence
is capable of proof.

Faith is the activity by which individual minds find themselves and establish a working association with the power referred to as Infinite Intelligence.

Day 238

All deeds follow thoughts. There can be no deeds without their having first been patterned in thought.

Day 238

One sound idea is all you need to achieve success. It is the average person's weakness to accept the word impossible, and to accept as fact the limitations they have in their own minds.

Day 239

Moreover, all thoughts have a tendency to clothe themselves in their physical counterpart.

It's not what you're going to do, but what you're doing now that counts.

Day 239

Day 240

I am the creator of all forms of human misery, the instigator of discouragement and disappointment.

Have you noticed that people who try to run other people's lives seldom do a good job of running their own?

Day 241

The drifter's pet alibi, with which he tries to explain away his undesirable position, is his cry that the world has run dry of opportunities.

Since your day has the same 24 hours in it as everyone else's in the world, you have the same opportunity as everyone else for the skillful use of time.

Day 242

Non-drifters do not wait for opportunity to be placed in their way. They create opportunity to fit their desires and demands of life!

Whatever the mind can conceive and believe, the mind can achieve. Success comes to those who develop a success consciousness.

Day 243

The law of hypnotic rhythm fixes permanently the dominating thoughts of men, whether they be drifters or non-drifters.

Wishing for success is not enough. You must have a definite purpose and a plan to achieve it, and you must act on that plan every day.

Day 244

Only the drifter would wish to dodge
the influence of hypnotic rhythm.

Day 244

You must have a burning desire to succeed,
and you must utilize all the power of your mind.
Do not allow yourself to quit, to accept defeat.
Your only option is success.

Day 245

The highest power in the universe can be used for constructive purposes, through what you call God, or it can be used for negative purposes, through what you call the Devil.

Positive and negative emotions cannot occupy the mind at the same time.

Day 246

You fear the Devil and refuse to trust your God, therefore you have but one source available through which you may appropriate the benefits of universal power, and that is by trusting and using your own power of thought!

Day 247

I have made it attractive to you to use the Power of Infinite Intelligence to attain negative ends, through greed, avarice, lust, envy, and hatred.

The majority of people are ready to throw their aims and purposes overboard and give up at the first sign of opposition or misfortune.

Day 248

Remember, your mind attracts that which your mind dwells upon.

Willpower and desire when properly combined make an irresistible pair.

Day 248

Day 249

To divert you away from my opposition I had only to feed you on thoughts helpful to my cause.

Prayer is your greatest power! Be sure to give daily thanks for your blessings and avoid asking only for what you think you don't have.

Day 250

I have allies in all walks of life, to help me in connection with all human relationships.

When the spirit of teamwork is willing, voluntary, and free, it leads to the attainment of great and enduring power.

Day 251

Who would keep alive the fear of the Devil if I subdued the churches?

Never do anything that you can get some other person to do better than you could do it.

Day 252

Who would serve as a decoy to attract the attention of people while I manipulate their minds if I did not have some agency through which to sow the seeds of fear and doubt?

Sometimes it is wiser to join forces with an opponent than it is to fight.

Day 253

The cleverest thing I do is to use the allies of my opposition to keep the fear of hell burning in the minds of people.

Day 254

As long as people fear something,
no matter what, I will keep a grip on them.

Any dominating idea, plan or purpose held in the conscious mind through repetition of thought and emotionalized by a burning desire for its realization is taken over by the subconscious and acted upon through whatever natural and logical means may be available.

Day 255

Nature forces upon the minds of men the influences of their environment which are stronger than the individual's own thoughts.

Great achievement is born out of struggle.

Day 256

Children are forced to take on the nature of all influences of those around them unless their own thoughts are stronger than the influences.

Develop an "I don't believe in defeat" attitude! There is no such thing as defeat—until you accept it as such!

Day 257

Nature sets up a definite rhythm for every environment, and everything within the range of that rhythm is forced to conform to it.

Day 257

Believe that you are not limited … that the only limitations you have are the ones in your own mind.

Day 258

Man, alone, has the power to establish his own rhythm of thought providing he exercises this privilege before hypnotic rhythm has forced upon him the influences of his environment.

Look at problems as temporary setbacks, stepping-stones to success.

Day 259

The person who thinks in terms of power, success, opulence, sets up a rhythm which attracts these desirable possessions.

Repeated victories over your problems are the rungs on your ladder to success.

Day 259

Day 260

The person who thinks in terms of misery, failure, defeat, discouragement, and poverty attracts these undesirable influences.

Your attitude toward problems, difficulties and adversities is the most important factor in overcoming them.

Day 261

Habit establishes one's rhythm of thought, and that rhythm attracts the object of one's dominating thoughts.

Day 261

All personal achievement starts within the mind of the individual—knowing your problem is the first step in finding the solution.

Day 262

Hypnotic rhythm is something resembling a magnet and that is why the poverty-stricken herd themselves in the same communities.

If you adopt the "I Will/I Can" attitude, you are assured of having the skills necessary to turning a disadvantage into an advantage.

Day 263

Hypnotic rhythm explains the old saying, "misery loves company."

Every successful man or woman, no matter what the field of endeavor, has known the that lies in these words: Every adversity has the seed of an equivalent or greater benefit.

Day 263

Day 264

Hypnotic rhythm also explains why people who begin to succeed in any undertaking find that success multiplies, with less effort, as time goes on.

A burning desire is a motivational force more compelling than wishing, hoping, and desiring combined.

Day 265

All successful people use hypnotic rhythm, either consciously or unconsciously, by expecting and demanding success.

Day 266

The demand for results becomes a habit, hypnotic rhythm next takes over the habit and finally the law of harmonious attraction translates it into its physical equivalent.

Day 267

Hypnotic rhythm cannot change the nature of the physical body one inherits at birth, but it can and it does modify, change, control and make permanent one's environmental influences.

Take control of your life and change whatever needs to be changed. You and only you have the power to do this. You can change your world!

Day 268

I may as well tell you that any human being who can be definite in his aims and plans can make life hand over whatever he wants.

You must intensify your wishes into a burning desire—and back that desire with continuous action on a sound plan.

Day 269

The opposition knows that definiteness of purpose closes the door of one's mind so tightly against me that I cannot break through unless I can induce one to form that habit of drifting.

Copy the following statement and put it where you'll see it the first thing in the morning and the last thing at night: I have a definite major purpose, and it is my duty to transform this purpose into reality.

Day 269

Day 270

I draw people away from definiteness with my promises.

Day 271

I attract people by feeding them liberally of the thought habits in which they like to indulge.

Your mental attitude is the medium by which you can balance your life and your relationship to people and circumstances—to attract what you desire.

Day 272

When a child is born it brings with it nothing but a physical body representing the evolutionary results of millions of years of ancestry.

Everything you need or want has a way of showing up as soon as you are ready for it.

Day 272

Day 273

If a child's parents fear me and express that fear within range of the child's hearing the child picks up the fear through the habit of imitation, and stores it away as a part of its subconscious stock of beliefs.

Cooperation between your conscious and subconscious minds gives you the ability to contact, communicate with, and draw upon the power of Infinite Intelligence.

Day 274

Once any person learns the power of his own thoughts he becomes positive and difficult to subdue.

Day 274

Never mind what others didn't do.
It's what you do that counts.

Day 275

Once any person hesitates, procrastinates, or becomes indefinite about anything, he is just one step removed from my control.

Say it with deeds and words will become unnecessary.

Day 276

I am bound to tell you that I eventually reclaim for my cause all who escape me temporarily through definiteness of purpose.

When you meet with disaster, use accurate thinking and a Positive Mental Attitude to imagine the worst that can happen, realize that you can survive whatever might happen and accept that as your new starting point!

Day 277

The reclamation is made by filling the mind with greed for power and the love of egotistical expression, until the individual falls into the habit of violating the rights of others. Then I step in with the law of compensation and reclaim my victim.

Boastfulness is generally an admission of an inferiority complex.

Day 278

Every principle of good carries with it the seed of an equivalent danger.

Keep your mind positive. Know what you want.
Plan your work and work your plan.
Go the second mile in all human relationships.
Move on your own personal initiative.

Day 279

All habits, save only that of the love of definiteness of purpose may lead to the habit of drifting.

If failure should overtake you, don't waste your time worrying about it. Instead, concentrate your efforts on finding the seed of an equivalent benefit and use it to your advantage.

Day 280

Love for truth, unless it assumes the proportion of definite pursuit of truth, may become similar to all other good intentions.

Good deeds are of more benefit than good intentions.

Day 281

Love is a state of mind which beclouds reason, will-power, and blinds one to facts and truth.

Develop a plan of action and act on your plan.

Day 282

You may be surprised to know that love is one of my most effective baits.

Wishing is not a substitute for action . . . you must take daily action toward your goal. Remember, success is achieved only by those who try—and keep trying!

Day 283

Love and fear, combined, give me
the most effective weapons with which
I induce people to drift.

People react according to the state of mind
you send out to them.

Day 284

Give me control over a person's fears and tell me what he loves most and you may as well mark that person down as my slave.

No one can make you jealous, angry, vengeful, or greedy—unless you let them.

Day 285

Both love and fear are emotional forces
of such stupendous potency that either
may completely set aside the power
of will and the power of reason.

Day 286

People who gain and maintain power must become definite in all their thoughts and all their deeds.

Day 286

Faith without action is dead. It is the art of believing by doing, coming as a result of persistent action.

Day 287

Definiteness of purpose plus definiteness of plan by which the purpose is to be achieved generally succeed, no matter how weak the plan may be.

A weak plan often succeeds through strong enthusiasm!

Day 288

The major difference between a sound and an unsound plan is that the sound plan, if definitely applied, may be carried out more quickly than an unsound plan.

The master key to success lies in your capacity to believe that you will succeed.

Day 288

Day 289

People who are definite in both their plans and their purposes never accept temporary defeat as being more than an urge to greater effort.

Day 290

Through the operation of the law of compensation everyone reaps that which he sows.

The quality and quantity of the service you render, plus the mental attitude in which you render it, determines the amount of pay you get and the sort of job you hold.

Day 291

Plans based on unjust or immoral motives may bring temporary success, but enduring success must take into consideration the fourth dimension, time.

Day 292

Time is the enemy of immorality and injustice.

Life's battles don't always go
To the stronger or faster man,
But soon or late the man who wins
Is the man who thinks he can!

Day 292

Day 293

The youth often makes the mistake of coveting the temporary gains of immoral, unjust plans, but neglects to look ahead and observe the penalties which follow as definitely as night follows the day.

A Positive Mental Attitude determines whether you act favorably or unfavorably, constructively or destructively, positively or negatively.

Day 294

Friction and all forms of discord between minds lead inevitably to the habit of drifting, and of course to indefiniteness.

Until you have learned to be tolerant with those who do not always agree with you—until you have cultivated the habit of saying some kind word of those whom you do not always admire—until you have formed the habit of looking for the good there is in others instead of the bad, you will be neither successful nor happy.

Day 295

The first duty of every human being is to himself!

A person with PMA aims for high goals and constantly strives to achieve them.

Day 296

Every person owes himself the duty of finding how to live a full and happy life.

Choose a "pacesetter." Pick someone prosperous, self-reliant, and successful; then decide not only to catch up with that person, but to pass him or her by!

Day 297

Parents owe their children everything
they can give them in the way of knowledge.

Remember that the mind grows
strong through use.

Day 298

The sort of prayer against which I am helpless is the prayer of definiteness of purpose.

There is no such reality as passive faith.
Action is the first requirement of all faith.
Words alone will not serve.

Day 299

Definiteness is in effect the only sort of prayer upon which one can rely. It places one in the way of using hypnotic rhythm to attain definite ends . . . by the mere act of appropriating it from the great universal storehouse of Infinite Intelligence.

Isn't it going a little too far to ask the Creator to do something for you that you could do for yourself?

Day 300

When you hear a person praying for something that he should procure through his own efforts you may be sure you are listening to a drifter.

What you do is much more impressive than what you say!

Day 301

Infinite Intelligence favors only those who understand and adapt themselves to her laws.

The day you adopt a Positive Mental Attitude is the day you will meet the most important living person—YOU!

Day 301

Day 302

Nature makes no discrimination because of fine character or pleasing personality. These things help people negotiate their way through life more harmoniously with one another, but the source from which prayer is answered in not impressed by fine feathers.

Day 303

Nature's law is, "know what you want, adapt yourself to my laws, and you shall have it."

Day 304

I thrive on ignorance, superstition, intolerance, and fear, but I cannot stand up under definite knowledge properly organized into definite plans, in the minds of people who think for themselves.

Definiteness of Purpose is the starting point of all worthwhile achievement. This means knowing what you want, having a plan to get it, taking daily action and not settling for anything less.

Day 305

Omnipotence and I represent the positive and the negative forces of the entire system of universes, and we are equally balanced one against the other.

Day 306

Every human being has a wide range of choice in both his thoughts and his deeds.

A man is born with some inalienable rights, but his privileges he must earn.

Day 307

Every human being can use his brain for the reception and the expression of positive thoughts or he can use it for the expression of negative thoughts.

Make up your mind today to be happy! The one difference between happy people and unhappy people is attitude.

Day 308

The only thing of enduring value to any human being is a working-knowledge of his own mind.

The human mind is a form of energy, a part of it being spiritual in nature.

Day 309

Ignorance and fear are the only enemies from which men need salvation.

A Positive Mental Attitude plays an important role in your health, including your day-to-day energies and enthusiasm for life.

Day 310

Teach all students how to recognize practical ideas that may be of benefit in helping acquire whatever one demands of life.

By repeating several times each day, "Every day in every way, through the grace of God, I am getting better and better," you'll be putting the force of PMA to work for you.

Day 311

Teach the students how to budget and use time and above all teach the truth that time is the greatest asset available to human beings and the cheapest.

If you learn to budget your time correctly, you will have time for all your needs.

Day 311

Day 312

Teach the student the basic motives
by which all people are influenced and show
him how to use these motives in acquiring
the necessities and the luxuries of life.

The happiest people are those who
have learned to mix play with their work and
to bind the two together with enthusiasm.

Day 313

Teach children what to eat, how much to eat, and what is the relationship between proper eating and sound health.

Day 314

Teach children the true nature and function of the emotion of sex, and above all, teach them that it can be transmuted into a driving force capable of lifting one to great heights of achievement.

Day 314

If you don't have the full approval of your conscience and your reason, you'd better not do the thing you're contemplating.

Day 315

Teach children to be definite in
all things, beginning with the choice
of a definite major purpose in Life!

Day 316

Teach children the nature of and possibilities for good and evil in the principle of habit, using as illustrations with which to dramatize the subject, the everyday experiences of children and adults.

Help your brother's boat across, and lo! your own boat has reached the shore.

Day 316

Day 317

Teach children how habits become fixed through the law of hypnotic rhythm, and influence them to adopt, while in the lower grades, habits that will lead to independent thought!

Only you have the power to do this, and it's easy if you know that the only difference between happy people and unhappy people is attitude.

Day 318

Teach children the difference between temporary defeat and failure, and show them how to search for the seed of an equivalent advantage which comes with every circumstance of defeat.

Close the door of your mind on all the failures and circumstances of your past so your mind can operate in a Positive Mental Attitude.

Day 319

Teach children that the human brain is the instrument with which one receives, from the great storehouse of nature, the energy which is specialized into definite thoughts; that the brain does not think, but serves as an instrument for the interpretation of stimuli which cause thought.

If you would plant a suggestion deeply, mix it generously with enthusiasm, for enthusiasm is the fertilizer that will insure its rapid growth.

Day 320

Teach children that there is a law of increasing returns which can be and should be put into operation, as a matter of habit, by rendering always more service and better service than is expected of them.

Day 320

Good intentions are useless unless they're expressed in appropriate action.

Day 321

Teach children the true nature of the Golden Rule, and above all show them that through the operation of this principle everything they do to, and for another, they do also to, and for themselves.

All anyone really requires to start a successful career is a sound mind, a healthy body, and a genuine desire to be of as much service as possible to as many people as possible.

Day 322

Teach children not to have opinions unless they are formed from facts or beliefs which may reasonably be accepted as facts.

The keenest minds are those that have been whetted most by practical experience.

Day 323

Teach children to encourage the use of their sixth sense through which ideas present themselves in their minds from unknown sources, and to examine all such ideas carefully.

The imagination is the workshop of the soul where all the plans for individual achievement are shaped.

Day 323

Day 324

Teach children that the space they occupy in the world is measured definitely by the quality and quantity of useful service they render the world.

The Quality of service rendered, plus the Quantity of service rendered, plus the Mental Attitude in which it is rendered, equals your Compensation in the world and the amount of space you will occupy in the hearts of others.

Day 325

Teach children that all school houses and all textbooks are elementary implements which may be helpful in the development of their minds but the only school of real value us the great University of Life wherein one has the privilege of learning from experience.

Day 326

Teach children to be true to themselves at all times, that they cannot please everybody, therefore to do a good job of pleasing themselves.

Day 326

Never argue over unimportant details. Even if you win, you'll have gained no advantage!

Day 327

Sin is anything one does or thinks which causes one to be unhappy!

There is a material advantage in being agreeable to other people. You will never be as happy in any other way as you will be when you know that you are making others happy.

Day 328

Human beings who are in sound physical and spiritual health should be at peace with themselves and always happy.

Day 328

Go out of your way to speak a kind word or render some useful service where it is not expected.

Day 329

It is a sin to permit one's mind to be dominated by negative thoughts of envy, greed, fear, hatred, intolerance, vanity, self-pity, or discouragement, because these states of mind lead to the habit of drifting.

If you are able-bodied, don't ever admit that the world has not given you an opportunity.

Day 330

It is a sin to cheat, lie and steal, because these habits destroy self-respect, and subdue one's conscience and lead to unhappiness.

If you can't forgive, don't ask to be forgiven.

Day 331

It is a sin to accept from life anything one does not want because that indicates an unpardonable neglect to use the mind.

Faith is the element, when mixed with prayer, that gives you direct communication with Infinite Intelligence.

Day 331

Day 332

Everyone has the potential power to clear his mind of all negative thoughts and thereby avail himself of the power of faith.

Faith is a state of mind that may be created by affirmation or repeated instructions to the subconscious, through the principle of autosuggestion or self-suggestion.

Day 333

Lack of self-mastery is, of itself, the most destructive form of indefiniteness.

A little job well done is the first step toward a bigger one.

Day 333

Day 334

People who eat wisely and keep their body sewers clean handicap me because a clean body sewer generally means a sound body and a brain that functions properly.

Eat right, think right, sleep right, and play right, and you can save the doctor's bill for your vacation.

Day 335

If humans would control their sex desires and transmute them into a driving force with which to carry on their occupation one half the time they dissipate in pursuit of sex they would never know poverty.

Day 336

No one can learn to think accurately without including, as a part of the needed knowledge, information on the control of sex emotion through transmutation.

Day 337

The habit of expressing loosely organized opinions is one of the most destructive of habits. The habit develops a grass-hopper mind—one that jumps from one thing to another but never completes anything.

Make good or make room, but don't make excuses!

Day 338

The person who talks too much informs the world of his aims and plans and gives to others the opportunity to profit by his ideas.

If you don't know what you want, don't say you never had a chance.

Day 338

Day 339

Wise men keep their plans to themselves and refrain from expressing uninvited opinions.

Day 339

The man who doesn't reach decisions promptly when he has all the facts in hand can't be depended on to carry out decisions once he makes them.

Day 340

There is no human being now living, no human being has ever lived and no human being ever will live with the right or the power to deprive another human being of the inborn privilege of free and independent thought.

Day 340

No individual has sufficient experience, education, native ability, and knowledge to insure the accumulation of a great fortune without the cooperation of other people.

Day 341

No adult human being ever loses the right to freedom of thought, but most humans lose the benefits of this privilege either by neglect or because it has been taken away from them by their parents or religious instructors before the age of understanding.

Day 342

Success usually is but one short step beyond the point where one quits fighting.

Day 343

I hate to tell you this, but failure often serves
as a blessing in disguise because it breaks
the grip of hypnotic rhythm and
frees the mind for a fresh start.

Day 343

True faith is applied continuously,
but it is tested at the time of your greatest need.

Day 344

Nature does not force people to fail. But nature does impose her law of hypnotic rhythm upon all minds, and through this law gives permanency to the thoughts which dominate those minds.

Successful people make decisions quickly, as soon as all the facts are in, and change them very slowly, if ever. Unsuccessful people make decisions slowly and change them often and quickly.

Day 345

Failure is the dead end of the habit-path one has been following, and when it is reached it forces one to leave that path and take up another, thereby creating a new rhythm.

If you can't do great things yourself, remember that you can do small things in a great way.

Day 345

Day 346

Failure often leads an individual to an understanding of the power of self-discipline without which no one could turn back after having once been the victim of hypnotic rhythm.

Day 347

Nature uses failure to break the rhythm of negative thought when an individual becomes improperly related to himself in his own mind.

Day 348

No one can change the law of hypnotic rhythm any more than one can change the law of gravity, but everyone can change himself.

Day 348

Time is a wonderful healer. It tends to equalize good and evil and to right the wrongs of the world.

Day 349

The sixth sense is the organ of the brain through which one receives all information, all knowledge; all thought impressions which do not come through one or more of the five physical senses.

Your five physical senses give you contact with the physical world. Your sixth sense operates through your subconscious mind and gives you contact with the invisible forces of the universe.

Day 350

Successful human relationships, to endure as such, must be formed of minds that naturally harmonize, quite aside from the question of having common interests as a means of bringing them into harmony.

Master Mind Alliance is two or more minds working together in perfect harmony toward the attainment of a common, specific objective.

Day 351

Adversity relieves people of vanity and egotism. It discourages selfishness by proving that no one can succeed without the cooperation of others.

By forming a Master Mind Alliance, you may acquire and utilize the experience, education, influence and knowledge of others to help you achieve your definite major goal.

Day 352

New habits offer the only way out
for people who fail.

Faith is a state of mind that you can
attain only if you condition your mind by
clearing it of all negative thoughts.

Day 353

Life gives no one immunity against adversity, but Life gives to everyone the power of positive thought which is sufficient to master all circumstances of adversity and convert them into benefits.

When a group of individual minds are coordinated and function in harmony, the increased energy created through that alliance becomes available to every individual in the group.

Day 354

All people absorb and take over either consciously or unconsciously the thought habits of those with whom they associate closely.

Day 354

A Positive Mental Attitude brings with it faith, enthusiasm, personal initiative, self-discipline, imagination and Definiteness of Purpose, which attract people and beneficial opportunities.

Day 355

Be careful of all forces which inspire thought, those are the forces which constitute environment and determine the nature of one's earthly destiny.

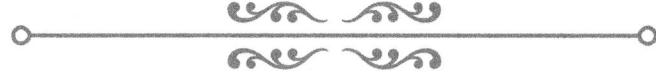

A Negative Mental Attitude carries with it fear, indecision, doubt, procrastination, irritability and anger, which repel people and drive away favorable opportunities.

Day 356

Every human being is duty bound to himself to remove from his environment every influence which even remotely tends to develop negative thought habits.

Day 356

Clearly define to yourself what you want to attain in life. Say to yourself: "I can do it. I can do it now."

Day 357

Negative thought habits control the individual and deprive him of the privilege of self determination.

Day 357

The first step toward a successful Master Mind Alliance is to get on good terms with yourself. This is one alliance you can't do without.

Day 358

All negative desires are nothing but frustrations of positive desires. They are inspired by some form of defeat, failure, or neglect by human beings to adapt themselves to nature's laws in a positive way.

It is the cooperation of the conscious and the subconscious minds that gives you the ability to contact, communicate with and draw upon the power of Infinite Intelligence.

Day 359

When the individual does not use the brain for the expression of positive, creative thoughts, nature fills the vacuum by forcing the brain to act upon negative thoughts.

Faith is the art of believing by doing. It comes as a result of persistent action and cannot exist at the same time as fear.

Day 360

Time penalizes the individual for all negative thoughts and rewards him for all positive thoughts, according to the nature and purpose of the thoughts.

Day 361

Time is nature's seasoning influence though which human experience may be ripened into wisdom.

Day 361

A group of brains coordinated in a spirit of harmony will provide more thought energy than a single brain, just as a group of electric batteries will provide more energy than a single battery.

Day 362

People are not born with wisdom, but they are born with the capacity to think and they may, through the lapse of time, think their way into wisdom.

Faith helps you to see your plans as completed reality, even before you begin putting them into operation.

Day 362

Day 363

Wisdom is the ability to relate yourself to nature's laws so as to make them serve you, and the ability to relate yourself to other people so as to gain their harmonious, willing cooperation in helping you to make Life yield whatever you demand of it.

Teamwork is the spirit of cooperation that allows individual members of a team to work together temporarily to reach a shared goal.

Day 364

In the realm of thought there is a time when it is proper to sow the seeds of thought, and there is a time to reap the harvest of those thoughts, the same as there is a time to sow and a time to reap from the soil of the earth.

Day 364

Exercise produces both physical and mental buoyancy. It clears sluggishness and dullness from body and mind.

Day 365

One's associates constitute the most important part of one's environment, and environmental influences determine whether one forms the habit of drifting or becomes a non-drifter.

Until we recognize the oneness of all people and the fellowship of all mankind, we will not be in a position to benefit from the principle of cooperative effort.

Day 366

Nothing contributes more to one's success and happiness than carefully chosen associates. Caution in the selection of associates becomes, therefore, the duty of every person who wishes to become happy and successful.

Day 366

Teamwork is sharing a part of what you have—a part that is good—with others

www.ingramcontent.com/pod-product-compliance
Lightning Source LLC
Chambersburg PA
CBHW052010070526
44584CB00016B/1686